I0517788

OWL

Poems

DAVID JOHN ROSENHEIM

OWL
Copyright © 2024 David John Rosenheim
All Rights Reserved.
Published by Unsolicited Press.
Printed in the United States of America.
First Edition.

No part of this book may be used or reproduced in any manner
whatsoever without written permission except in the case of brief
quotations embodied in critical articles or reviews.

Attention schools and businesses: for discounted copies on large
orders, please contact the publisher directly.

For information contact:
Unsolicited Press
Portland, Oregon
www.unsolicitedpress.com
orders@unsolicitedpress.com
619-354-8005

Cover Image: Nancy Lu Rosenheim
Cover Design: Kathryn Gerhardt
Editor: S.R. Stewart

ISBN: 978-1-963115-00-0

Acknowledgements

These poems are dedicated with love to Jackie, Oliver, Judah, Animal, mom and dad, my four sisters, and to the quiet of the Dell.

Deep appreciation to Nancy Lu, both for the wood cut "Owl" and for a lifetime of art. Thank you to my teachers Maya Stein and Heather June Gibbons, as well as to my editor Maw Shein Win. Deep bows to my Zen teacher, Marc Lesser, and to the Bodhisattvas down the line.

I am grateful to the following publications, which have published some of the poems in this book:

Adirondack Review
Americal Journal of Poetry
Apricity
Avalon Literary Review
Broadkill Review
The Banyan Tree
California Quarterly
Common Ground
The Dew Drop
Frigg Magazine
Grief Becomes You
Madison Review
Midwest Quarterly
North Dakota Quarterly
Painted Bride Quarterly
San Antonio Review
The Sandy River Review

Poems

I

II

III

IV

OWL

I

Sonoma

light rotates
morning to noon
olive branches sway

meatheads in the pool
drink vodka lemonade
bees work the lavender

the wind drops
American flags shrug
and go limp

children wrinkle
in chlorine
summer moves on

super-moon rises
over rows of grape vines
sign of a good year

Mendocino

The ocean unrolls from the window
Boys wrestle sheets on the pullout
Rocks froth the clean waves wheeling in
There is talk but no decision on the day

Boys wrestle sheets on the pullout
Birds converge in V's; it is November
There is talk but no decision on the day
The soul contained slakes the open sea

Birds converge in V's; it is November
Last night's wine rings the toppled glass
The soul contained slakes the open sea
Empty the hook rack, vacant the car park

Last night's wine rings the toppled glass
The boys, now settled, coo over glowing screens
Empty the hook rack, vacant the car park
River's mouth discloses a lone swimmer

The boys, now settled, coo over glowing screens
Rocks froth the clean waves wheeling in
River's mouth discloses a lone swimmer
The ocean unrolls from the window

Dylan Beach

this perch
views mouth of
river and sea
windless pink dusk

   must be something in it
         tea cup of rye
                hum of highway one
                        bruising horizon—a question?

the Swedes are chatty now
softened by cuba libres and hours in the hot tub
they've evolved to store heat

fruit flies find everything we eat, and drink,
mosquitoes find us too, the soft parts around our ankles and
arches the puppy lurches dumbly at house flies

you feel like crying because there aren't enough carrots for the
soup because you feel strongly but can't put words to it
we can remember all of this

  I am trying to write the present not prescient
                        find the is, as Spicer
                            not the image

    I have questions, there are things I want to know
    but keep forgetting what to ask

Joshua Tree

Joshua trees crackle as they
release their heat into the gloaming

lizards' electric chirps relay
between the granite monoliths

stars radiate in luminous spokes from the dome

coyotes stamp at the ground and howl in the ecstasy

their voices reverberating through shafts of long forgotten
silver mines

ghosts of prospectors, once wanton hang in the carbonic air—
wanting still

a bobcat drinks languidly from a small pool
her eyes, the water, the firmament form a close symmetry

Falcon Heavy

Marina Blvd
manicured lawns
harbor swaying
against the old Fort
in the weak light
of a winter morning

Today Falcon Heavy
made the grade
but Major Tom still spins
his sad tale in endless spider webs
across the exosphere
his frozen ghost ever watching
the electric sizzle of a world
whose economies
burn too bright

Clones run purebred
pups on Marina Green
while Earth dries out
on a string

Major Tom's circuit is long dead
and I am older than all of them now

but these green sprigs
pushing through my toes

don't ever quit
push, pushing toward
the cold eye of the sun

Lake Willoughby

last day of summer break
Lake Willoughby
primal mountains
rising from crystalline deeps
sunlight slowed
filtering through
308 feet of blue

fields of black-eyed Susan
lonesome loons calling across
the mirror
dead pine reflection
a portal

boys learning to skip
every stone tossed
a tempest of ripples

today we fold
this expansion
into two suitcases

tuck the flaming birch
bone cold lake
percolator coffee

into the cups
of our children's memories

Lodestone

The shadow of Mount Cook
leans across the wash

Darkening the flat yellow grass where
morepork and plover

Garble their language
backward as the seasons

Of this southern land
they drink snow melt and

Fish lamprey from glacier-blue pools
they buzz the scrub

Making their business as if
the mountain held no majesty

As if the mountain were not the lodestone
pulling forth the tempest to come

Vernazza

You write the same scene
over and over again
but cannot get it right
memory demurs as you examine it

The tart burst of apricots
as you eat them one after one
from a blue enamel bowl
figs too, their tiny seeds
popping between teeth

Three round tolls of a distant church bell
all of this under a lemon tree
hung with fruit so heavy and bright
they remind you of lanterns

And the placid sea yawning toward the horizon
beyond the terracotta rooftops of the village
water so blue that the thought of it
still makes you soft with longing

All the skiffs are in, the fishermen
ensconced in cool rooms dreaming
the afternoon air so warm and thick
even the bees have quit the lavender

She is dreaming too
her Italian Vogue folded on her chest
her shoulder tan and sculpted
you kiss it and then her neck

The taste of salt and
the faint smell of sun cream
overwhelm you
overwhelm you still

You retrace these images again and again
but cannot be certain it was Vernazza at all
the sea or a mountain lake?
A blue bowl or green?

You will never get it right
you cannot raise that ephemeral bloom
only the pining, the grasping remains
you hope someday to forget all of this

Milos

I put my wife and boys
on a boat off a southern beach
my stomach is no good on boats
the wind was down
the sea flat and green

Later, the wind rose
a single bell tolled
from the Byzantine tower
cicadas sawed from a bent eucalyptus
in the church square
but I don't believe in omens

Tonight, after my family
have rinsed the salt and
sunblock from their skin
we will eat our last dinner
on Milos
wine, olives
scorpion fish

Who knows what change will have come?

Udaipur

A pigeon perches on a ledge
just outside the open side window

My eyes are closed
but I'm sure of it

She cranes her purple neck
in little jerks to see into the room

Sniffs at the prospect of food and smelling none
she is gone in the dip of a wing

Below the sweeping sound of the street
like wavelets on a gravel beach

Inside, far inside, you are asleep
dreaming away the sickness

That kept you in hot sheets
a day and two nights

A string of sandalwood beads between us
we are very far away in place and in time

The Ganges closer than the Kickapoo
and everyone wants to go home

But in this window of our lives
we have no home to return to

Perhaps we never will
maybe we never did

And still your cheek sleeps as ever upon the pillow
the boys' soft ears fold between my fingers

Rishikesh Minefield

Sitting here is
a minefield
of distraction

Someone snores
another shifts on her pillow
creaking leg bones

I get a breath in
maybe two
my son twitches

In his skin beside me
from the heat of his being
and last night's mosquito bites

I exhale and my hips hurt
the room is too loaded to focus
it's Monday somewhere

The guru has returned to Rishikesh
from his mission in Manitoba
to kindle spark in wilting souls

Many have gathered
in pre-dawn murk to drink
warm milk from his lips

Our familial pod has blown like a seed
to the banks of the Mother of all rivers
the deepest turn in our journey

And still, I cannot awaken.
A monkey on the Ashram roof bends the tin like a madman

I elongate my spine
into a meat-string of pearls
a cockcrow wind rushes

Down the Ganga valley
mirroring the texture
of the water's surface

Its eddies and rapids
its dark green pools
like the season are turning

White City

A small domed window
welcomes in the lake air

still cool from night
the smell of cardamom and aniseed

the palace city
white city

its king, still asleep
dreams morning dreams

brought to him by birds already at work
pigeons, parrots, king fishers

before the weight of his
76 generations

of fore-king-fathers
presses upon his temples

his warrior horse
long at pasture

this king owns hotels
builds schools

oils the mustaches
that are his birthright

he watches, watches
the placid ripples

dreams of the fire
that will boil his lake

and melt his marble
walls like butter

Bangkok

a tree grows through the open roof of the café
ferns and orchids drape low and heavy with bloom
over conversations closely held

by pairs that make no notice of
the surround sound: squid frying in back
a saw cutting metal down the road

their consonant chatter in
interweaving languages whose meaning
you can only sense by tone and inflection

a bent man, a monk, you think
brings you tea that softens your veins
you are a conduit now

a dangling rope bridge, between.
more sounds:
dishes in sink water, a distant bell

arrive and exit as clouds
the immediacy of it lifts
your heart to your throat

like a flock of birds
riding the heat, the exhaust
of the human city

Isthmus

Thailand is a wall of water
the low tide mud percolates
dreams from the underworld
mangroves expire monkey breath

Yesterday in Bhubaneswar
you thought the sky was raining
rickshaws and crocodiles
airplanes have a way of

Disinfecting the past but
people in these old lands
understand the weight of salt:
blood, breakfast, promises kept

We went to the isthmus with
our bags of laundry,
half smiles, half loves and
coddled fears scratching the roof like rats

A storm shouldered in
between the limestone cliffs
yellow on the edges
mad purple within

We were in hot water
spouting in long arcs like whales
rolling back to belly and back
when the first drops fell like cold bells

And then the curtain came down
by the time we reached Joe's Bar
the sand path was a flash flood
swirling around our calves

Past and future wiped clean
only sweet rain in our eyes
turning our speech to garble
and then the lightening!

A full squall transfiguring Earth
into a poultice of herbs
sewage and drowned beetles
turning our fear into pure, liquid joy

Vietnam

They're playing that tinkly music again
Ice skating in the hot broth of a tropical storm

Everything is different here
Motorcycle traffic swirls like ballet

Beneath apartment blocks that march
To the horizon like teeth

Fish sauce for breakfast
The children get it—

Skating with mascot penguins and seals
As if   as if

The ground water don't flume Agent Orange
Or mountain uncle's skin weren't plastic smooth

Where his eye sockets should be
Playing victory music for tourists

As the nation's blooming youth
Build chrome spires to happy pink heaven

On the gold fillings and bone dust
Of their merciful kin

The Sound of a Fountain in Mexico City

Pigeons flap
through the chemical haze struggling
for elevation

a girl's shriek, horn blast or
Bedlam at the Gate of Lions
sparked the exodus

Chapultepec.
Concrete ensconces the soft ground like a corset
the alien form of the mushroom fountain
drips and seethes

I sit at the transom
cleaved open by the sound of running water

Tizoc's legions once streamed
across this red earth
soft padding of a thousand feet
insects buzzing like wood saws in the green gold air

I sit in a hanging chair
drinking coffee as ever
air plants cling to branches

"And all times are one time"
the old pulse still quickens
blood still iron and salt

Rakaia Gorge

Somewhere in NZ
a green rain
pines lording over
the tempest river

Clean country here
the four of us quiet
huddled by a stream
stewed by seven-months

On the road
a thin connection
as if through static
to the life we once knew

We are soft as kiwi now
rolled in the camper bowl
loosened by the world
its poor and

Open-hearted villages
its old temples
returning inch by
inch to dust

Ready at last for home
where we hope
nothing has changed
and everything will be different

Journey's End

Every morning the rain falls somewhere
Perhaps on the hot hills of Udaipur
Where it washes ragged feet only Gandhi would kiss
Or Milos where it bores the lunar cliffs
Into eye holes that watch the fishing boats
Rain falls in the fiord lands
Releasing a thousand waterfalls that
Weep vainly at their own majesty
And this morning it rains in Queenstown
Curtains of silver and gray on
The dimpled face of Lake Wakatipu
A quiet breakfast before a long journey home

II

Kettle

in the morning
you move liquid
between vessels

the bed table glass
empty but for
a finger of water

silver in early light
the kettle, shaking
hissing

as you pour
the tea
anxious

morning is like that
the prickle of dread
as we remember our burden

steam wets your face
as you douse
the coffee grounds

Swarm

Sunday, as we climbed
the stairs from the beech
below the old fort
dripping with lake water

our familial pod
was ambushed by
a swarm of wasps
choking our exit

wrist, neck and thigh
ballooned and cramped
the venom took
hours to unclasp

this was no accident.
Mom told me a woman
was found dead at dawn
that same beach

her husband, a suspect
911 at 4am
his bed empty
sand in his teeth

Morning Holies

Holy the morning
Soft cheeks of sleeping boys
Eyelashes in half-light, holy
Holy the early tinctures
Hot lemon water and black coffee, holy
Holy the woman in starry tunic sleeping
Holy, holy
Holy black dog stretched on midnight blue quilts
Holy birdsong and commuter traffic
Holy the scratch of pen on page
Holy the quiet
Holy the rage

Conflict

The intimacy of it
your wet breath on my face
the heat is turned up
and in some way, so is the love
you, gorging on anger
like chocolate cake
your lips shaking, spilling with it
me, slapstick in my
naked monkey shame

We love each other like that
the fools gold moon
shimmering in sink water
through the open window
bats flexing and puffing across
the actual moon

The crucible of truth spoken
a place where transfiguration can happen
a new language
for things we dared not
feel or speak before

Boundaries

Last night we were souls in charcoal
or watercolor smear
afraid of letting go
of our separate selves
the clear edges of our selves
but we did let go
smearing, blurring our boundaries
as we joined the melee
spiraling upward and around
dissolving into fractals
blurring, rising
toward a great union
a yoking

this morning you left
the door ajar
a slice of sound
from the kitchen
wedging in
tea kettling
butter spattering in pan
the baby cooing

you brought coffee
a pen and pad
and we sat to set our list
reconstitute the things we know to be

the year
the spring this day
the things we will do
the gentle borders
that remind us of who we are
alone and together
for these dear
these numbered days

Empire

Your grandmother Blanche died
In an oven tomb
Birmingham, Alabama
Foreshadow of Birkenau
Her husband's coagulated heart
Looping in her thoughts as
The Plathian gas bid her sleep

Your father was a man on the outskirts
At least in how he saw others seeing him
Selling appliances for dough
Keeping up appearances at the club
Until the cold shock of self-annihilation
Gripped his jaw
Then his hands
Then his mind
In uncontrollable shaking

I forgive them.
Of course I do Do you?
Their tender souls

Dancing as candle flame
Same flame
Same flame

But we don't speak of them
When pressed, the memory is frail
As a gauze of dust
While our hearts and tongues
Memorize heroic tales
Of stronger ancestors
Builders of empires
Captains of steel and grain
Stock we still hold for safe passage

Speak now of the unspoken ones
The smudges on the edge
Of our memory, the shadow
The door-to-door sales
Each rejection
A small humiliation
The oven, even
Yes the oven
Speak their names
Blanche, Harold
Invoke something of their habits, their music

A tie clip
A Handel sonata
A tortoise shell comb

Speak their names
To bring balance to
To our empire
Which, after all is only sand

Breaking in the foam

Let it crumble
Let us be free to dream
Not of Sears or Paramount
But of bread and friendship and love
A game of catch
The flicker of light
Touch of skin
A familiar voice in the gloaming
The warm bricks of empire
The only empire we have

Villages

You have seen this village before
the beer hall and inked stained arms
the come-down twitch of a boy
whose eyes you have also seen
as he looks up from his task
of picking litter off the street
then sanitizing his hands
from a vessel of Purell
carabinered to his pack
rubbing his knuckles until red, then repeating

There is another village
by a cold river
where life also hangs in the balance
beneath towering rocks
that sometimes fall at night and
circling vultures pass the sun like a clock
their nature to wait for death

You want to take him there, the boy
to cool his chafed fingers
among the troutlings
unclasp his brow
in resonance of bells
pulsing in the valley

The old 71 bus kneels with a hiss
taking the man, now bent
to another corner to clean
in another village

I am Odysseus in my Bed

In one dream
chased by wet black dogs
running down steep ravines
barbed wire crossings

It's early she says
sipping hot lemon water
can we talk about James?
but I am in ravines

Cutting my way to the sea
the gorge is steep and
dark falling to
places unknown

I am Odysseus in my bed
when the northerly blows up a swell
our house, a ship cast in mist and foam
salt licking at the door

I am nobody
to those who would speak my name
nobody to the chorus
I am nobody and I am free

The old family clock awakens
after a century or more
hands spinning back
back past the births of my sons

My marriage
my punk rock days
my fat boy pain back, back
past the narrow straights of my own birth

The dogs lick their paws now
resting by the crackling fire
their oiled fur and curled teeth
glistening in the glow

The clock slows its backward whirl
stopping in the boat
that brought it here
black coal smoke

Streaking across the Atlantic
smudging the harbor sky where
soot-winged gulls relay their kill
calling their code across time

Cow Barn

cow barn
blackbirds spiral
from a vacant window

children wade in
shimmering creek
jeans stuck like
second skin
hurl rocks at
electric wire

cows steep
in cool rushes
downstream

barn swallows, pigeons
start from the hay loft
at a slammed door

a boy
tentative
aware
his pace slow as
sunlight trapped in honey

I scoop him up with one arm
breathe his neck
his yellow head of hay
we lock pulses
his heart-blood
floods me
I am his servant
this blue-gold child

Neighbors

Hand clap echoes
4am
thigh slap acoustics
garbage can

warm milk bottles
left on stair
blue fur grown
no one there

pain chips chewed
windowsill
burn rubber squeal
squashed daffodils

back seat baby
change of plan
hand clap ricochet
garbage can

mail piled high
from Tarrytown
hook on line
dangled down

lips silk membrane
easy to read
puffy, punctured
let it bleed

lips drink milk
sour, spoiled
suckle earlobe
secret told

shoe in swamp
toe to sky
black cloud rumble
mail piled high

back seat sweatbox
6 am
thigh slap symphony
garbage can

Fixer Upper

In this house
the ghosts are busy
guarding their turf:

> web strewn boiler room
> mystic night lawn, steaming
> dead Debby windows

a woodpecker clucks a hole
in the awning where one phantom leaves
its blank eye to watch us growing up

> shooting imaginary Nazis from the tree house
> coffee on the porch at dawn before a flight to San
> Francisco mother bent quilting by lamp light

sometimes the ghosts take action
but it drains all they've got
their shrillest howl

arrives as only a
twist in a dream
your eyelids jitter as the

> black panther's fur you stroke
> turns to golden floss
> she paws your beach ball

making you jealous
you try to take it back but
the ball transfigures into

a squealing vulture
and you wake
in wet sheets

Roger's Park

my sister's studio
heat wave
Rogers Park
her knife glides through
cold papaya
she squeezes lime on
the pink flesh

her city garden tiger lilies
orange petals curling
 each leaf offers
a single seed
onyx teardrop

Lu's studio
crowded with
fantastical forms
colossal
jellyfish
veins
ova

jars of pigment
line her workman shelves
explosive colors

pthalo blue
ultramarine
paynes grey

open tubes
of paint
release in the heat
spilling their portents
rose madder
purple lake

it's a hot night
a fan churns the
watery air
blurring the lamplight
and the edges of our
teeth and skin
our personalities run like
milk as they converge with the night

Maidenhair

After a tough week
I find myself in your care
Your shade, a grace
Old Maidenhair

You arrived years ago
Before the children came
In a blue plastic cup
From Paxton's Gate

Raised among spiders
Web-dappled sunlight
Fountain-dribbled song
Gargoyles' watchful sight

Then bought and sold
A house-warming gift
For a house gone cold
A quantum of green

I didn't know—had to learn
How water and light
Sway you so, my feeling fern
Voices too, move through you

And now, your soil wet
May's late day sun tilting low
Leaves like infant hands
Forgiving, unroll

I, my tea, my pen
Am a novice in your lee
I have only to breathe
Green thing,
Bodhi tree

Maelstrom

Winter storm warning:
a gray plaque
centuries-long

Moves in from the Pacific.
You drank too much last night
your wine-soaked tongue let him have it

Another lecture
on the flawed man he is becoming
every barb, a stitch in his husk

Disengaging, I set the cruise control
for the long sweep up the hill
cranked up the Zeppelin

Later I smoothed his brow with my thumb
then told you I loved you as we lay in silence
my throat thick as wet wool

I dreamed of a forge
the alchemy of ore and fire
but G-d knows I can't fix anything

This morning
I slipped out into the dark
as the first drops fell

A terrible wind mounted Laguna Street
while I sat dutifully on the cushion
struggling to empty the bucket of my mind

But it was little use
trying to understand the beginningless origins of
all my twisted, ancient karma

Tatami

A clean morning on Haight and Fillmore
octopus arms uncurling off the canvas
black coffee and cut lilies mist the air

Even the 7 bus kneels toward Golden Gate Park
as if conjoined in convocation
as if that moment isn't already

Gone. A certain death
one of so many today
the flies buzz-diving the trash can, dead.

Bananas in the produce stall
slow death of fruit decay
rotting fecund in own skin

Dead a million cells of my spaced-out brain
or my aging, freckled arms as I shake them out
a gentle snow on the dead wood floor

My fathers and mothers down the line
dead this moment or the next
hopeless heart cracking like a sparrow's egg

Craven slurp-sucking yolky marrow til gone
dead gone as the expanding exhale of
deep empty space between cells and stars

It's okay, let's not be sad about it
it's the great revelation, the ultimate relaxation
think swimming pools and movie stars

This death and dying everywhere
every breath a death
a chance to wipe away the residue, clear sight

And O the living sounds
car alarm temple bell WAKE UP!
sound of breath catching throat

The mystic whinny of spoon
in cup conjuring a cyclone
of tea and cream

The sternum punch thud of surf
every wave crest a death
never to be repeated

Today I took a vow
with shaky knees
on the tatami

To die and live and die, a swinging door
as the endless purge one
by one crosses over

III

Full Summer

rain came early and strong
now the season is thick
bugs cloud the woods
bats and swallows at night
cows, neck high in grass can't keep up

children drink
mouthfuls of cream
before bed
lay in hammocks
dream of owls
grow inches at night

in the day they jump from trees
into the crooked river
one boy, blond and sunburnt
gashes his sole on a tree root
blood flows between
his fingers, clutching foot

he cries but knows
this too will soon mend

a hawk spirals
up on a draft

farmers mark the
towering corn

Steuben Song

Dreaming of Steuben again
The hearth the heart the blood the bell
We smoked corn silk
We ran the hill

All the creatures laying still
The snow lay thick upon the ice
The blade cuts through
Enough to skate

We clear a circle to look through
A frozen fish's silver eye
Looks from me to you
Looks from me to you

Carry wood to light a fire
As our ancestors survived
The sky is streaked with cold starlight
Spinning on this lonely ice
(Spinning on this lonely ice)

Dreaming of the sea once more
Far below the burning plane

Baptism of salt and foam
I hold you in the turning waves

Back in time the river slow
Voices echo through the woods
Horses pull till wet with steam
Sticks are snapping underfoot

Clouds amassing from the North
The fear of cold awakes the spine
To pump the blood to raise the barn by dusk
Neighbors arms are strong and just
Neighbors here are generous

      Dreaming of the sea once more
      Far below the burning plane
      Baptism of salt and foam
      I hold you in the waves

But O to skate the Steuben lake
The pulse below that Steuben lake

Unincorporated

Barnum, unincorporated
shoulders a bend
in route 171
backed by steep hills

crowded with
chokecherry
blue ash
jack pine

a thorny, buzzing prairie
stretches opposite the road to
the mud bank
brown river

almost a town
one general store
abandoned
windows and corners
swathed in web
jars and cans
U.S. one-gallon jugs
entombed in silt
ancient notices
yellow, brittle
litter the floorboards

three or four houses
buckled
sloping
junk in the yards
one by the road
white
pallid
luminous
shifts in shadow
of the hill's lee

a girl in the
upstairs window
rocking, mouthless
the sky xanthic, darkens
flocks of blackbirds rise
like darts from the scrub
wheeling
across the wan sun

her eyes wide
fixed, imploring
collide indelibly with mine
as I ride East

Edna Larson

No salt scrub
nor chemical peel ever
shined that face

not Edna Larson
only the cadence of
94 summers and
93 winters

one cow farm
round hills
misted valley
every summer night
a symphony

the good farm lost to
a tornado in '38
hand to mouth for seventy years

alone in the
howling winter
old walls bending

still awake at four
relieve the brown cow
knotted, powerful hands

milk spits
into tin pail
steaming

The Road Divides

One road rambles:
spring fed shallows
cranes knee deep

Hum of the bog
Queen Anne's Lace
beloved master

Master love
hand-scooping cold
mouthfuls from the

Moon-shimmered well
honey skin
hymn sung

Lain on wet sod
with downy lips
and opiate eye

One road descends:
the roan mare
foaming tongue

Wild eyed thirst
empty saddle
dangled boot

Mad padding hooves
through glacial ravines
and gnarled vines

Overcome with scent
the blood, the boot
the matted nape

Road of suffering
ruined outpost over
Johnson Creek

Egg drop sun
twitching nostrils
spectral silos of

Waterloo
the corn had no rain
in June

(sing)
'O the quarter ye have found
Upon the old blue mound
Six digs of soil and for ye toil
The cold black ground'

Geography (Instructions for Pearl Hunting)

You sense the call until
half mad with it
you scramble through
berry thorns and nettles
to the splintery ladder
hoist yourself up
nine rickety steps to
the Doug Fir planks of
the old tree house

fill your lungs with steam
and look North
scan treetops and furrows
an oval of cows below
a solitary turkey vulture circles

if you follow that spiraling bird
you will see town kids
calves smeared in mud
dive off a picnic table
into the river

hands stuck sand bottom
bodies suspended as constellations
in the brown swirling plasma

that's where you lose the trail
under there in the silt where
the blind and tentacled slither
where, half-buried
a knotted muscle shell
its crooked jaw
and algal tongue under which

a glowing pink pearl
pulsates a signal
you cannot see
and you will never decipher
but are called to again and again
from your vaulted green spire

Bees

You have been at market
collecting bees in your pockets

bribing them with lavender blossoms and lunch meat
their soft wings like kisses on your wrists and neck

you bring them home day after day
but alas, they never stay

their heart is with the swarm and
that old woman next door has made a deal with the Queen

they can hive in her walls if the Queen's minions
promise to carry her soul sunward when released

now the swarm labors and drones
between the studs behind her bed

30,000 bodies warm her brittle bones at night
she sleeps away her last days in a house made of honey

Twenty

last birds of day
frogs, crickets, katydids
owls relay
down valley

sacrosanct
rolling orchards
riding today
apple and cherry

rolling orchards
prayer at 20mph
prayer at 20mph

brown skinned
the boy
myself the priest

brown skinned
the boy
invocation to teach

myself the priest
old enough
last birds of day fade

Lynx

Miles of country road
a lush green gorge
dark comes too quickly
for night, an eclipse

as if G-d has
put a thumb on the sun
to up the stakes
of this game

your game
you pass a
towering dead elm
its branches bleached
white as whale bones

in a crook
a dozing black lynx
lifts her head
her yellow eyes

stare you down
you remember your torch
but its light
is swallowed whole
by the pressing night

you wake far from that valley
a rare June rain
taps the skylight
like fingers on a drum

Pineapple Sage

behind my right ear
I hear the choked chirp
of a hummingbird

the helicopter patter of her wings
as she extracts serum
from the narrow chutes

of pineapple sage
growing red and bombastic
in an unkempt corner of the garden

fork-tongued leaves of artichoke
crowd the weathered arm
of your Adirondack chair

sunlight on the
side of your face

bramble towers overhead
unfurling white blooms
like peace flags for embattled bees

bored as ever
you put down your book

the chard we planted last winter
is running now, a great effort skyward
its clockwork belling in the time to seed

you have abandoned your chair
shutters slap against the windblown door

I inhale as the evening fog sweeps in
for too many years I have not tended this garden
for so long I have paced my heart

is this what has driven you away
matching my distance inch for inch? we are both complicit

let's agree now
to dirty our fingernails
in the business of love

to squish the slugs
chase the cabbage butterflies
reeling upward from

our small square of sky
let us nurse the worm bed
for it is the soil and the bread

Campervan

You open the side window and
birdsong floods the van
there is a pause in the rain
you take our son to pick tart berries
staining your teeth

staining your teeth
ferns along the river
unfurl around your ankles

Earlier, you climbed to the lip
of an old blue glacier
the last of its kind
melting like candlewax
into the southern sea

Your yellow poncho
a flag in the storm
ice calves and waterfalls
fed the foment as you
disappeared beyond a rise

I boiled ramen for the boys
on the camper stove
our long johns wet and stuck

to cold chicken skin
the van windows gathering steam
we wiped away

we wiped away
scanning the horizon
for your return

IV

OWL

there is one thing to do
before you leave
go down to where the marsh
has overtaken the old pasture

past the crumbling
barn veined in ivy
and the tilting silo

sit on a bank of sand there
or on a slow-rotting log
in the clear reflection
of the evening sun
gold light on your face

listen for the owl
that you have long traced
but never seen

that ancient voice calling
your wood born soul
to rise
let it print its code
on your neck and heart

giving you what you need

to leave this time
leave because the living road requires it
leave again so that you may return

Garland

Grief is a garland around you
in the way you dance in the kitchen
making chocolate cake
one moment and the next

You are on your back tears
shining their way to your earlobes
five-months now since your dad
died too young and broken hearted

The way your intuition
unmasked itself those final hours
knowing exactly what to do
how to forgive, when to let go

Today we eat a spring lunch while
a hummingbird drinks from sage blooms
you are not alone in grief, love
though he was left and riven

Your heart is big and holds him now
holds us all and the pain too, pink as a new scar
big as a field of poppies
the purest thing I know

Loom

As we sit together
the old and the young
a silver thread is looped
each breath
is an end a pause
a beginning
so is this circle
of generations complete
no ardor left to bare
just sitting together
even across the miles
the digital expanse
as black birds cry
in their spring dew home

Ascent

After the mechanics of preparation
a moonlit departure
pine needles crunching underfoot
wood bridges over whitewater
four birds on a pine bough
first light at tree line
fields of snow corn, scree
shedding layers
the sun breaks over
camelback ridge
short breath, ringing head
pitch after final pitch
finally the wind alone bellows
Tibetan prayer flags

Echo Lake

Open your eyes
to the vast pine gorge
silver morning light angling through

Let your spirit scream
across snowy rocks
the thawing edges of Echo Lake

Leave your body
an empty shell
if it does not understand

Let it drink its coffee
or build a fire
as your true nature

Old quiet one
the eye, the crown
races crows

From treetop to granite crag
to the icy depths
of the volcano bowl

Anything is possible
in this limitless geometry

The distance between
clouds or stars
an exhale, a dive into

Every belief you clutched
as a blanket to chin
that in the end became a burden

Dissipates in the prickle
of rain spit on your cheek
sunburst across your ribs

Gathering

My mother
the older she gets
allows gaps in
her speech
a soft place
where thoughts gather
or memory tugs

As the house passes its hours
the furnace stokes and withdraws
small clicks of floorboards
expand with the heat

The soft padding
of her slippers
pauses as she stands
in the hallway
trying to remember
what she is moving toward

Outside the fall sky
stacks layers of cloud
silvering the low sun

For long stretches
the quiet is marked only
by the furnace, the floorboards
and mother retracing her steps

Bloody Knuckles

your stomach ripples
as if you swallowed the
buzzing phone
that bore the missive
"baby, I'm gone"

a sound like a
bulldozer beeping
springs from your gut

you look surprised
as if you don't know
you're about to blow

an old memory flashes—
the Canada girl
see-through skin
blue veins
the lodge
in Banff
lead panes
wracked by
sheets of
Arctic rain
cracking fire
piled high
dogs asleep

on bear pelts
as after medieval hunt

playing
knuckles
with her cruel sisters
loser's penance
full deck slap
you held
her hand
the first time
her soft
child skin sticky
with blood

the beeping accelerates like
card flaps against bike spokes
you hold your breath
squeeze your eyes and
wait to detonate

Finishing Touches

of a summer sojourn
the water park
a last poem
lunch with Jill
hard chested and
bent onward
armored against the
claw of ancestry

until Rosewood Beach
the lake's clarity

wooden guard chair
in skeletal silhouette
on the empty beach

a gathering on
water's edge
a memorial as

each in turn
with a word or gesture
seals the life lived
Viking sea burial

Going

open window

still, humid night

late train rumbles
northbound from Chicago
everything is easy
here fridge stocked with
fresh OJ
whitefish salad
expired condiments

Wednesday
time to go
back to
certain fog
Pacifica, CA

every time
every damn time
I leave as if the first
Dad weeping silently
Super 8
Canton, NY

John Boat

at the big pond, father and sons
a heron turns its blue throat
takes flight at a falling branch

the John boat, bottom-up
in lake sand, decades have passed
lichen on the hull

in the flood of '78 as a boy
he speared walleye with pitchforks
now capillaries of cracked mud

Leaving

You slept in the lee of a saguaro
the dawn when a plane nosedived into

the desert floor waking you with
tequila eyes to the twin red balls

of the flaming metal cocoon
and the actual sunrise

you, rising on stiff knees
unsure which was your fault

implicating yourself in the drama as usual
as streams of birds flew like arrows

or souls, you thought
from the scene

leaving, you thought
everyone is always leaving.

Homecoming

The house is as we left it
blue vase in the kitchen window
lemons in the bowl

But I forgot how to unlock
the closet door where our secrets were kept
and which pillow is mine or yours

Are the daffodils coming or going?
The birds appear exotic, new to the neighborhood
the old walls seem moveable, transient

As if they could collapse into the floor without warning
exposing a view of a new world
an open air tree house in the green light of Earth's curve

The dog drops
a toy at my feet, waiting
at least she remembers who I am

Before we left, I hid a stone from our garden
in the suitcase, a token of home
to carry across the continents

A moveable hearth I take now
to plant in the artichoke bed
a new journey begins

Why I Cry On Airplanes

It's Tuesday and the century is still new
I am on a plane, hurtling from LA to San Francisco
there is a commercial on TV
something about a Chevy truck, a farm, a homecoming
I cry as ever on flights—I don't know why
the thin air maybe
or fact of leaving
loosens me until I am soft with
thoughts of you, the boys
fear of change and aloneness
but also beauty—the symmetry of nature
any half-wrought Hallmark sentiment
in magazine or on TV
will give rise to the ache in my throat
I don't like the way these things make me cry
though they often do

the sea below a brilliant matrix of
sunlight and shadow
Channel Islands sit like jewels caught in gossamer
each a world within a world
alone but infinitely connected
this too chokes me up

the sky mingles with space at this height
its blue becomes indigo
closer to bright moon and stars

those burning, self-consuming stars
who, like us began as sparks showered into the blackness
(before which we were one)
those cold stars
who awakened the ache in ancestors
the ache of separation that
makes me ache like a hollow gut-drum

I remember the pillow soft grass
above Lake Michigan
my first love
her tongue tart with wine her
leg bones wrapped around me the first time
this sweetness too aches because it is so far gone

from here the brown hills of California
an endless rippled sea
the ache of these hills where
as young men we lost our way hiking
ran out of water
our destined hilltop pool
but cracked clay and fish bones
we nearly expired that day
the furnace of August
our heads singing from thirst
the sky bruised with crows
I press my forehead to the plastic inner window
the great American highway below
vein-work of the California corpus
the 5 begets state highways

county roads
rural capillaries
the road makes me ache—its constant yearning
you—the country lane
somewhere between Memphis and Wisconsin
salt of your neck
even then the ache of our souls converging
the ache of intimacy

we begin our descent
trees and buildings gain definition
proximity of home
the ache of arrival
strangeness of reappearing in one's life after being away
arrive—leave—arrive—leave
my children grow in bent time
the ache of impermanence
my love transfigures
we lurch toward the city at unnatural speed

About the Author

David is a poet, songwriter, and novelist based in the San Francisco Bay Area, where he lives in a solar-powered house by the sea with his wife and two boys. The Weather Band, Hugh, and Winchester Revival have released his songs on seven critically lauded records, and his poetry has been published in many fine journals. David is a student of Zen in the Soto tradition and seeks connection with others through writing and music. David is a graduate of Oxford University, is a seasoned entrepreneur and leadership coach and is focused on fighting climate change and building a sustainable future for people and the planet.

About Unsolicited Press

Unsolicited Press is based out of Portland, Oregon and focuses on the works of the unsung and underrepresented. As a womxn-owned, all-volunteer small publisher that doesn't worry about profits as much as championing exceptional literature, we have the privilege of partnering with authors skirting the fringes of the lit world. We've worked with emerging and award-winning authors such as Shann Ray, Amy Shimshon-Santo, Brook Bhagat, Kris Amos, and John W. Bateman.

Learn more at unsolicitedpress.com. Find us on twitter and instagram.

www.ingramcontent.com/pod-product-compliance
Lightning Source LLC
Chambersburg PA
CBHW031439120626
46545CB00006B/2478